TREE LANGUAGE

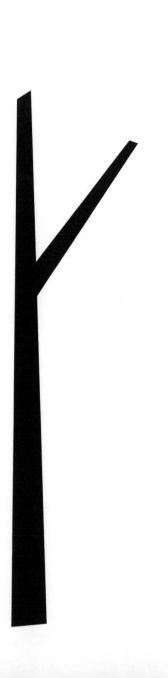

TREE LANGUAGE

EYEWEAR PUBLISHING

First published in 2014
by Eyewear Publishing Ltd
74 Leith Mansions, Grantully Road
London w9 1lj
United Kingdom

Typeset with graphic design by Edwin Smet
Author photograph Somerled McCready
Printed in England by TJ International Ltd, Padstow, Cornwall

isbn 978-1-908998-24-8

WWW.EYEWEARPUBLISHING.COM

For Jamie
Sorley and Ruby

THE 👓
MELITA HUME
POETRY PRIZE

Marion McCready is the 2013 winner of the Melita Hume Poetry Prize. The winner received £1,000 and publication by Eyewear Publishing. The 2013 Judge was Jon Stone. His citation read:

'The poetry is incredibly dark and rich and bloody (blood is a particular theme), with frequently brilliant lines and almost Celan-esque word pairings: 'blood-cut son', 'snow-eyes dressing', 'death fruits'. As a collection, it's superbly structured. Repetition within and between the poems is used to haunting effect; often, a motif or image returns in the manner of a memory resurfacing, or a recurring dream. The loosely held themes allow her to cover a range of territory, including war poems, over four distinct chapters, without seeming to stray from the direct path established in the opening pieces. This is assured, disconcertingly potent work with a sharp and distinctive flavour.'

Marion McCready was born on the Isle of Lewis and brought up in Dunoon, a small town by the Firth of Clyde, where she currently lives with her husband and two small children. Marion studied Politics and Classical Civilisations and an MLitt in Philosophy, both at the University of Glasgow. Her debut pamphlet collection, *Vintage Sea*, was published by Calder Wood Press (2011). McCready has received the RSAMD Edwin Morgan Poetry Prize and a Scottish Book Trust New Writers Award (2012/13).

Table of Contents

Where the Dead

and the dead in Christ shall rise first
1 Thessalonians 4:16

Clever Elsie

I
They say it's a gift
but I didn't ask for it –

to see the wind
rolling up the street,

to have ears so attuned
as to hear a fly cough.

And if that wasn't enough,
there are the premonitions

of my yet-to-be-conceived son –
a pickaxe dunting his head.

Is it any wonder I need my rest?
Out in the cornfields,

the drowsy golds of the harvest sun,
bowl of broth warming my belly,

I lie down, close my eyes
for one sweet moment.

II
I wake to dark fields, caught in a bird net,
dwarfed by corn stalk silhouettes.
Am I alive or dead, animal or woman?
Crashing through the fields, shrill bells in my head,
I batter my knuckles on the familiar window
of the familiar house. "*Hans, is Elsie there?*"
The words leaving my mouth like steam from a kettle
and then the reply – "*Yes, yes she is.*"
The street shrinks to a series of small doors;
the wind is coming. I run, shedding feathers,
flies coughing all around.
That's when I saw him, my son,
my dead son, whom I had not yet borne,
standing there, staring, his bloodied face
footage from a distant war.

Arrochar Alps

I have been known to birth a mountain whole,
a range of them in my belly;

I popped them out one by one.
The blood-cut son born black,

I could not believe the wholeness of him,
the crushed diamond of his face.

And then another,
who flew from me, a shooting star;

a twin mirror girl, whose orchid face
opened and opened and opened.

There were more of them –
one born of water, one of fire,

one for every element.
But now my mountain days are done.

The red night clouds, the afterbirth,
the snail shell whorls of them.

The unborns we named:

Beinn Narnain, Ben Vane, Beinn Ime,
Ben Vorlich and Beinn Bhuidhe.

I love him like an oak table

so solid and Plato. His lips, two candles
lighting and lighting.
The chorus of my crab-claw tulips
bubbling, their red gowns floating
from the plastic vase.
The wine glasses drain from our wrists
as he rests like a tree trunk
curved into our high-backed, high-loved chairs.
Drink up, my love; supper is over.
Tomorrow the cock will crow.

Cursed

Still life, still death.
The sun sets in blood-red whirlpools.

How foreign the blood-clouds look,
as though they belonged to Mars or Jupiter.

On the hill, a burning bush.
Arms catching the sinking smear

of the gold-ring sun.
Arms of the unborn, whose own cellular ring

flushed from my womb.
A *ring of hope* he called it,

on the black-and-white screen.
We three ticketed to your debut,

to your no-show.
Probably for the best, he said.

As if the Brahan Seer
had cursed our offspring.

Winter Girl

A triptych of birds
erase themselves from the scene.

She stands on the bridge,
not one but three.

Trees on land, trees in water;
everything reflecting, multiplying
surrounds the Erinyes.

A cut-out girl, a frozen river.
The meteor-snow flashing
into tarred water.

She is the blackness of stones
under a snow-bomb.

Leaf-shaped sky
glitters between treetops.
Black hole on the horizon,

her legs, her coat,
hair rising, river body.

Snow-eyes dressing the forest,
ice drifts, an extension of her gaze.

The sparse grasses reach gingerly
and the dead trees flail:

ghost ships of winter,
return of the Erinyes.

The Black Art

The black art of the shore
strokes the gills behind my ears

The black art of the shore
rises around us.
Mussels crackle-comb the air,
rocks jostle with sea drift,
our conversation takes place
in my hair.
I am a lampshade of a girl;
I light up the rocks
with the whirl of my skirt.
You may think I am a sort of fish, you may
stroke the gills behind my ears.

Drovers' Loch

Munro and Corbett
climb into each other's pockets,

birthmarked by tree patch
and sun-tattooed.

The sheer blue of the laundered sky.

The brute cry
of the drovers' oxen

as they ferry the cattle
across the loch.

Thick skins blackening
and glistening;

cloven hooves swimming
through plankton, fossil coral,

peacock worms.
When the darkness comes

it brings with it
an oxen moon.

Which is the memory bank
of the land.

Where the Dead

Cloud-shadows darken the windows.
    In an upstairs room I watch the city glide by.
        The gulls have followed me to Wet Paint city, where you live,
            in a Fairtrade sky.

Bloodied, wing-bent,
the white-backed gull runs
dragging its hung limb.

★

Berry-reds burden the thin air
    in the hills above the Clyde.
        She has a calling into the darklands,
            tumbling through the air... the taste of seaware rising...
            the parachute of her hair.

"Ma mam, she's as high as a kite
an ma nan, she's finished wi' me.
Ah'm sorry... Right?"

★

Daffodils, pale, washed out rags.
　　Ivy-wrapped trees. The rail track, a waste ground,
　　　　a derelict graveyard. They exhume bodies
　　　　　　to build a road.

I left you in peatland,
marsh-moor and the Minch,
where the dead in Christ shall rise.

The Clyde

breathing, two streets away,
writes its reverberations on my bones.

Spidery fuchsias
drag through my hair,

the flat heart leaves of autumn
skirt the road.

Tiny fern hands
reach out from the walls

and the doll
in the pram is smiling

as the brittle edge
of a shorn hedge

scrapes at my elbows.

Conifer barracks
stalk the hills.

I move round puddles,
the pallor of death

and the blinking monochrome
of a magpie rests,

Buddha-bellied, on my head.
One for sorrow.

The Animal in the Pot

She was browning the animal in the pot –
by 'the animal' I mean meat.
And a young girl was screaming in the next room –
by 'screaming' I mean singing.
The sun was spitting crystals through a window,
through the leaves of a basil and a poinsettia
she had managed to coax back to life.
The pot sizzled with blood and scum
as she turned the dead meat with a spoon.
The screaming girl in the next room
was also no longer animal
but a young woman who was singing.
The basil remained as did the sun-crystals,
but the poinsettia, having lost its Christmas reds
and summer greens some time ago, was mere memory
and could only be coaxed back to life in the mind
like the animal before it became meat,
and the screaming before it became singing.

Fatras

I

Above us, the bellies of seagulls
on the window by your bed.

Above us, the bellies of seagulls.
Everything duplicate in shadows:
blackbird on the aerial, the luminous mosses,
your broken words, half-spoken sentences.
The scrolls of your eyes...
You advise:
"Don't look at a new moon
through glass or water"
         and
"Place a psalm of David
on the window by your bed."

II

The mountains are scalloped with snow,
pheasant wings beating in the glovebox.

The mountains are scalloped with snow.
Water glittering through a dead hedge.
Sunlit gorse, downy birch, the Holy Loch
dragging its hair east of the estuary.
"I see the crows of Ardentinny"
you said, as we drove through the hollow of the road,
trees touching above us,
pheasant wings beating in the glovebox.

III

She pares her nails into cracks in the wall
uncommitted to breath.

She pares her nails into cracks in the wall
and reads poems to a dead poinsettia.
The wood burner in her chest,
kindling of her ribcage,
is fired by the word-birds unspoken,
uncommitted to breath.

IV

Standing in the loch, waist-deep,
and the wading hills drawing her in.

Standing in the loch, waist-deep.
Curls of dull light, her white dress
with its band of orange skirting the water.
The clouds closing in on her.
Brittle branches make obeisance at her side,
sensing the suck of the freshwater loch
and the wading hills drawing her in.

Rhubarb

growing in the corner of the garden.
She tends to it the way some women
treat their dogs like substitute children.
Nightly, she listens to the pop of bulb,
creak of stem, rhubarb crowns
breaking through the shoddy.
In daytime, she sees in every leaf
the continent of Africa,
each with its own Cape of Good Hope.
She has adopted the likeness of rhubarb,
taken to baring her pink arms and legs,
clothes exhaling the familiar tang
wherever she goes.
Then, when picking day comes,
she releases the stalks, one by one,
from the rhizome with a twist-and-pull
the way some women compulsively
pull hairs from their heads.

Four Poems

I
The thin wrist
      of my hydra-tree.
      All cartilage and bone,

exposed nerves
      to the bare wind.
      Flutter of knuckle-buds

growing
      from the centre
      of my garden.

Daffodil embryos
      clutching at the air,
      sea grasses whipping around us.

II
I watch the kindling-men
eat themselves.

The yellow candour
of the flames,

the calm animal of it,
tame

through the white-hot
transparency

of this telescopic tunnel
into nine circles of hell

in my living room.
The four bodies bow,

burning.
I watch the kindling-men

eat themselves
into ashes.

III
Red tower topped
    with beacon tea light.
Red cocktail,
    slice of lime climbing
over the lip of the glass.
The sails of your elbows
    pointing towards me.
Blue checked sleeves
    of your arms unfolding.
Our hands navigate
    the pine table, meeting
below the lighthouse
    of the candle, rising
above the lava
    of the cocktail.

IV

I don't know where I am
　　any more.
　　　　When I try to imagine my garden,
　　　　　I can't think of it.

Blackbirds, black stones,
stilled movements on the snowfields.

An alphabet of wing shapes.
The cut-lip berries, blood-crumbs.

The silver falls of her hair
sliding down her back.

The slow arc waves of her arms,
an underwater tree.

We'll always be... here for you...

Like a dead shrew

the baby lies comically still

its paw-hands curled above the blanket
its cold nose

the stopped pram sits without sound
without cry

she stands alongside it   dark-haired
dark-eyed

trapped in the picture
the father fades into himself

like a Gormley statue

underneath a zigzag of flags
cutting up the sky

she loves it   she loves it not
she loves it   she loves it not

Brambles

strangles of them cling to the gate
then they come towards us   multiplying in the air

creeping up the street   the fragile weights
of these hooded Furies

are everywhere
like postcards from the past

death fruits   bloods of Christ
the unpicked ones

harden on their arching canes

all late summer
we fed on the purple tears

The Pond is an Unknown Force

Ice scrapes a warning on its surface.
A dying signal, a hint of foul play.

The grainy ether floating beneath
hides a multitude of sins.

A submarine perhaps, a conger eel
or a sea monster with a thirty foot neck.

But more likely, the pond holds your body.
Pneumonia-bitten, preserved

in your hospital frost-gown.
I see you now, rising

to just below the surface.
Sleeve-wings spreading, waiting

for the ice to melt.

The Unintelligible Conversation of Unpicked Rhubarb

Silver rain flies through tumbleweed trees.
Black-eyed brambles are knocking at the door.
The babies lie, three, on the dining room floor.
One named Forty and one named Four.
And the other, face down, is no more.

Tree Language

Those who are willing to be vulnerable move among mysteries
Theodore Roethke

Roses

There is no escaping the storm of roses
crisscrossed on the split-cracked wall
of a dead fountain arch.
There is no escaping their uterine balls,
expanding as a reminder of the children I never had.
If you listen carefully you can hear the vibrations,
the heart drone of their petal jaw-harps.
And there's no going back,
no indiscovery of Mars
or these red planets brooding before me,
light predators, sun-hatched
and bloodening like the fists of women
who have gone to war.

Daffodil horns

                    star-splayed
mouths from the yellow bellies
of starfish   flat and helpless
mouths   unshuttable   though mute
unstoppable   culled from our garden
these lampshade-and-bulb trespassers
periscope from the bottom of a foreign vase
though we listen   we do not hear
though we see   we do not understand
and the daffodils   they spread like cancer

Water Iris by the Canal du Midi

I, who am more useless than corn stalks,
border the canal with my yellow tongues.
Though you barely feel my lips' touch
they are warm as the afternoon sun
blessing your cheek. You may think I am weak,
baffled hourly by the wind.
I embody the wind
and though I bend I do not break.
I release my flags, my fleurs-de-lis,
like incense into the calm of the canal,
into its brown hesitations.
And when my light fades
you will remember my movements
like the memory of someone
you used to love.

Wild Poppies

And how do you survive? Your long throat,
your red-rag-to-a-bull head?

You rise heavy in the night, stars drinking
from your poppy neck.

Your henna silks serenade me
under the breadth of the Pyrenees.

You move like an opera,
open like sea anemones.

You are earth's first blood.
How the birds love you.

I envy your lipstick dress.
You are urgent as airmail, animal red,

Ash Wednesday crosses tattooed on your head.
Your butterfly breath

releases your scents, your secrets,
bees blackening your mouth

as your dirty red laundry
all hangs out.

Tree Language

Cassiopeia-shaped grove,
tree-heads brushing the sky.
The split lightning of sun-cracks
between continental clouds.
Brightness unbearable
streams into my eyes.
Branches, pen and ink scribbles
of an unknown alphabet
twenty feet high.
Handprint of wind-chill,
record of fish-life,
root, bark and seed twitter,
the wishes of gulls.

Two Daffodils Lying on a Window Ledge

Yellow birds, dive-bombed, stunned.
They inhabit my window ledge
taking it hostage to their foreign bodies,
their green stick legs.
What am I to do with this invasion,
contamination of my pretty
little home-space? Dumb faces,
watching my every move.
They're under lock and key now.
Though I can hear them breathe,
lying there like a childless couple.

Basil

Pirate-basil, one-legged pot,
black.
Your green-coat swordsmen
collide, crash
like some kind of Peloponnesian War
or kids pile-on,
daddy slumped at the bottom.
Climbers,
you plant your brash flags
mid-air,
moon-conquerors.
Silent victors, sedate occupiers,
all the while
growing scorpions in my brain.

Night River

Oriental fire-flows,
   watery golds, candlelit reds.
      The river stretches its silks,
its peacock tail,
   to the yellow-tongued banks
      of the Gourock hills.
The pier, lit by oracles,
   orange balls,
      whose reflections
form multiple
   sea horses of lights,
      pointillism, in the shallows
         of the Clyde.

Edwardian Postcard, Dunoon

The punk-black Firth.
A single ketch cruising,
mizzenmast abaft the mainmast.
Then the Waverley, punching its steam,
punctuates the air with smoke signals.
Clothes, the colour of bladderwrack,
loiter on the pier's timber planks
beside the tiled, plumed pavilion.
And Mary, standing back,
bronze Fury of the Firth,
her unaltered gaze, blazing,
beacon for a distant lover.

It was Resurrection Sunday and

we sat beneath
the barnyard clouds.
The Gantocks, submerged,
but for one hunchbacked rock
sailing next to the broad thumb
of the lighthouse.
Some way up the Firth,
between mainland and Arran,
a ferry, hesitating,
the tail of Bute
sliding into the water.
Blue veins etch
through the milk carton sky,
snow-crumbs harden
on the Gourock hills.
All the while we waited
for a miracle
and the hooded daffodils
scarcely opened.

Gateway to the Highlands

Teal hump of Argyll, whaleback.
Hackles raised to meet the sky.
A nosedive cloud sinks to land.
Shoulder to shoulder they glide
into waves. Eyes drawn
to the river-ides,
the month of Clyde,
tide-Tuesday, fish-o'clock.

Ground Memory

A cocktail of March snows, coat-tails of winter,
ground-memory of manna.

A deckchair left out,
a wood-carved bear three smiles wide.

Trees create a cityscape from the snow-fogs.
The helter-skelter flakes

caught in the green wings of our garden.
Clouds hatch, crown us.

Comets spinning from a collision of seasons.
First, the tiny spears of snow-rain.

Then the flurry of white jackets.

The wishbone tree

is making cathedral shadows
on the ground
high arches stamped
on dirt   twig and stump
abbey peaks triangulating
sun-carved   unenterable
the dark forms   dead
to the roots of the tree-bone
that is their shape-maker
forked author
and alter ego

Transfiguration

Three stones stand
>*between sea wall and pier*

Three agèd men
>*barnacled, shell and crust-laden*

Three stones stand
>*mute in the galloping breakers*

Three agèd men
>*the Atlantic in the hollow of their hands*

Three stones stand
>*locked under clouds and their progeny*

Three agèd men
>*dreaming in the skirling gales*

Three agèd men
>*transfigurating in the sea-vines*

Three witnesses
>*Spirit, Water and Blood*

View

Marble sky indented,
swithering branches.
A pyramid of roofs,
the windows of Mary Street.
Rosemary needles rising
from a Belfast sink.
Lead strips carving
diamonds on the window.
The green wings
of a stained glass thistle
spill to milk cartons,
cereal boxes, a dripping tap
and the anarchy of shoes
as they proliferate
across the red tiled floor.

Plant-Heart

Hyacinth,
head full, falling.
Pink morass,
spine lowering you gently
in an arc. The spider-ants
of your dead flowers,
a last clutch of baby curls,
monkey hands, peach fuzz.
The dried-up bloods drip from
your dried-up plant-heart.

Orchid, One Year On

A pink nose
on every speckled
frost-flower.
Buds tendering the branches
bursting into butterflies,
badges of honour.
The veins in my wrists
reflect this network miracle.
Vital organs, delicate
and yet they grow
against the odds
découpaging my window.

Promised Land

Everybody has two cities, his own and Jerusalem
Teddy Kollek

The Green Line

At the foot of Mount Sodom we swam
towards palm trees and Japanese kasa
beach umbrellas.
Here in the valley of salt and light,
our son creates waterfalls.
The canopy, his sky, the pool,
a blue eye in the desert.
The sun warming my wet hair,
sun-waves christening my skin.

The Damascus Gate crowns us.
Soldiers fluttering between ash and spice.
In the souk, row upon row of rose water lokum,
comfort of the throat.
The sweet-wrapped cubes, little gifts
unfolding in our hands.
Dome-sun, the air floats with jewels and scarves,
hot pomegranate stings my lips.
At the garden tomb, the alcove eyes,
faces coming out of the stone.
Shadows of trees, branches,
the doorway, a mouth.

Tel Aviv, *daughter of the sea*, where,
legend has it, the fish kiss Adam's rock.
Out of the sun-plains, the white city rises.
Spring mound of life birthed by kerosene lamps,
a bible and a gun. "I will bring them
out of the north country
and gather from the outermost parts".

The wailing trees of Yad Vashem
(the people are coming home),
the hillside stuccoed with grave markers.
Gold star ceiling, the dark walls,
raw-amber lanterns like lit cigarettes.
The iconostasis of your face
(peace I leave with you,
my peace I give unto you).
An olive grove in the centre of Megiddo,
hands reaching out from the rocky ground
(the very rocks cry out).
Hands of hope, hands of blood.

The engine is still warm
in the mangled car in front of me.

A rocket fired over our heads –
hardly anyone at the school flinched.

A bus explodes under my office.
He only knew how to smile.

We became as the Golan Heights
after Yehuda Amichai

we became as the Golan Heights
dipping into each other

your eyes   crab-brown
Galilee boats   wood floats

tearing through holy water

we conquered the Beatitudes
orange scrub   livid as hellfire

hypnotised by the riddle of the sea
we looked over the blue eye of the Galilee

until the lights of Tiberius
choked into colour   stilled fireworks

on the shoreline and we became
as the Golan Heights

dipping into each other

Portrait of the Old City, Jerusalem

I
I don't see her face, only the tight red curls and outstretched,
bangled arm waving a flag under fish scale windows. In a small
stone tavern, at precisely 2.40 pm, mint leaves open in a glass under
my lips. Stepping up to the ramparts, turret-clouds imitate the
stone jigsaw of the walls, gravestones on the hillside glow gold
in a sun-stream. The flashing blood of brake lights multiplies up
the road, the Zion Gate Brailled with bullet holes. Inside a blue
door, stone steps ascend below a crescent window where lead
hearts curl.

II
The church and the soldier frame each other
as though asterisms in the Old City constellation.

A scroll of headscarves rainbow a tunnelled wall,
one man pointing, the other sitting with a nervous smile.

The ceiling speaks Ottoman, the ground, Roman-red polished stone,
veined with blood-memory and footsteps.

In the distance, three men run.
Freeze-framed they become, uncannily,

the three on a hill where the penitent one
turned to the other in supplication.

At the end of the tunnel, light gathers in a bright ball.

Candle-flowers open up their flames in a row.

The men stand out from the walls.
A trick of photography has them holding hands

and the afro-trees lean in like women.

III
Tooth-turret walls injure the skyline.
I am counting stones under the globe of a street light.

The Jaffa Gate gapes, half obscured by a tree.
White taxis line up inside.

A bird is caught on the downward stroke
and the casual stance of the soldiers forms vav's in the street.

Window balconies, black frowns on the love-stones.
Every window, an alcove, darkened and mirroring.

The walls growing, like coral fish, inside of them.
The arrow-slit-eyes of living stone.

IV
On the Via Dolorosa he sits on a white plastic chair,
talking on his phone, hands gesturing.
An upheld palm, prayer-like and a young man,
adjacent, and looking the other way.
Camel. Centurion. Archangel. Map of Jerusalem.

On the Via Dolorosa are shadows of minarets.
Barbed wire and broken glass circle a house.
Police barriers on the sidewalk, the writing on the wall
in Hebrew squares and Arabic curls.

V

High arches and bread carts. A couple rest, sipping water by twin
doorways. The promise of domes rises over the wall. Tapered
candles bow into limp shapes. Glass grasses kiss in the heart of
the Citadel (she smashes a figurine as a curse on the city).
The white slopes of the Mount of Olives. Domes, towers and
cupolas transform into olives, poplars and palms. The Judaean
hills undulate on the smoky horizon.
A lizard wills itself into a crack in the wall near a bricked-up gate
called 'Beautiful'.

VI

He sits under a palm tree, dressed in black,
sun-darkened and eating by the rotting

Corinthian columns of the Cardo.
They are beating swords into modern art.

Menorah-hands wave at the window.
Stone upon stone, the memory-markers grow.

From the dead wall, green clouds hang.
Under the olive and east of the palm

he phones home as the doors close
on the golden dome.

VII

The men in their black coats gather.
Their hats, ringed planets,
tilting ahead of them.
A walled up doorway has buried its crimes.
The narrow maze of Jerusalem stone
hangs on our shoulders.
The ridiculous giraffe-necks of the palms
converse at the city gates.
The blue sky dims into mist and behind the New Gate
a straggle of flame-clouds lower on the hill.
A minaret-arm stretches out of the city.
A plaza of palms all in a row,
the cross-legged olive, windswept.
Shadows talk in a rooftop garden.
The cross wires of the tramline slitting the sky.
Two ancient love trees joined at the roots,
one leaning east and the other leaning west,
red flowers bleeding into white.

O Jerusalem, Jerusalem...
how often would I have gathered you.

Song of the Jaffa Gate

Hot sun   hot stone   sun-caught
illuminate   the city waits

enter in through my arch
through my sleek bend you turn

mother   father   daughter   son
I am the herald of Jerusalem

mother of stone   birdsong wall
folded prayer-tears endlessly fall

they sell bread at my feet
taxi through my elbow

I meet myself within the Jaffa Gate
where I wait for you   my friend

Reflections

Sans songer: suis-je moi? Tout est si compliqué!
Jules Laforgue

Black Swans

Blunt-beaked, bloodshot-eyed,
their rump feathers singe the sky,

crook necks rising
to the ghost of a rainbow.

They spill across buttermilk waves
under the gaze of kouroi plane trees

who buffer Pyrenean gusts
and shoulder the grape-black sun.

This bitumen colony
ploughs towards me,

wailing from their liquid throats,
punctuating a sunbelt of water iris.

The black swans are nomads.
Tarred, feathered and, like me,

a long way from home.

A vision of Sula Sgeir

guano rock
shawled by the Atlantic

freckled with guga
a gulp of birds troubling its air

the gannet skerry comes to me
a dark calling

I float through its caves
glitter of gneiss   the open tide drift

sea thrift   luminous as coral
glows around the bent backs

of the guga hunters
and the crack of gannet wings

as feathers singe and sing
above the peaty blaze

they turn towards me
webbed feet

contorting in the heat
the heart of a cormorant

beating in my chest

Floating

leaves glitter above me
daylight fireworks
I imagine her floating
down the Clyde
hospital gown
fanning out around
carrying her past Bute
Arran   the Ailsa Craig
and everything around me floats
the yellow ring of gorse
the birch leaves flickering
on and off

Ashes

I comb my hair
with dried seaweed.
The black pods of it,
like blood clots,
catch
so that even a gale
able to auction off my dress,
if it so wished,
could not move
these signatories
of the sea;
or the yellow flag iris
on the machair,
or your ashes
from under the earth.

Charity

The shop is a valley
of second-hand clothes.
I carried off
my dead mother's scarves.
They lie with my baby
's first jumpsuit,
first Christmas dress.
Hands rummage, hangers sigh,
all around the material cries.
Second-hand clothes
have a song of their own;
it goes "for all men are like grass…
and the grass withers."

Seanair

Every inch of the worktops smothered in newspaper and on
top of that, salmon. The steely fish waiting to be sliced open. I
watched her scale them in the mouth of the sink; bending over
them, halving the glitter-bodies, fingers wrenching the guts. Out
of the window, the long slope road to Traigh Chuil, cupped by
grass cliffs, scattered with sheep-coats. The sky, cloud-blistered,
hangs low on the back of the croft. The door opens. You enter,
in blue overalls. The breath of the Minch rising from your skin.

Arabic swirls

over the wine rug.
    A fairy tale castle opens,

crab-like, on the floor.
    Glass hands carve
        an unlit candle in the air.

A bodiless dress
    languishing
        over the arm of a chair.

Morning comes
    as a young girl shawled
        in dressing gown,

peering into
    an exotic kingdom
        at lives unravelling

before her
    and under her
        crab-like hands.

Orchid

An anemone opening
under the sea,

flowers floating,
branches coveting the air.

I feed them to you secretly,
orchid tubers,

stirring the crushed bulbs
into your teacup.

And how they grow in me,
the white petal-stars.

Your eyes, now Tiffany lamps.

When we kiss, orchids
fall from our lips.

The Girls

Chubby palms smacked flat out on the table,
uncharacteristically patient and composed
with their necklaces, badges and rainbow hair clasps,
they admire the tide of nail polish bottles before them,
the limitless possibilities of the colour pink.
They watch their hands transform into something beautiful,
their tipped fingers glowing like lit matches.
Tools to provoke other girls to envy,
to feel glamorous though they don't know what glamorous means
or the years of chipped polish that lie ahead of them
or the dresses that will one day consume them.

Fork Kiss

The cutlery sings mouth-songs
from the metal filling of my cutlery drawer.
Stainless steel bones.
Grey-gleam, knife-beds, spoon-dreams,
horizontal coffins separate them.
I lift a fork to my lips, your bite
closing around the mirror-prongs,
meeting mine.

Reflections

I
broken bones   storm trees
hieroglyphics on the skyline

the ghost of a hill
enlarging across the Clyde

estuary

how beautifully sail the ships
we have missed

II
the snow hill rises   a peplos angel
we are walking towards it   walk

we are killing ourselves daily

the white crest of the hill
foams before us

at the end of the road
at the end   of the road

III
sea-burned shingle bound by bladderwrack
the men   casting their nets

their bodies twist   turning
into light then shade   fishing for ghosts

blood-rock humps hide a shoal of ships
sailing on the seabed   blazing

with plumose anemones

sea jellies bloom in my hair
my eyes   two orange buoys

warn on the horizon

IV
magnolias   silken birds
lie on the frost-taut grass

we exchange mist with our mouths
your lips canvassing mine

in dreams   the sea uncharts me

its tottering blacks call

the blood-waves are coming
the blood-waves   widen

the March moon rises out of my hair

Notes

'Clever Elsie'
Based on the Grimm's fairy tale of the same name, sometimes translated as Clever Alice.

'Winter Girl'
This poem is for James Owens.

'The Black Art'
Written in the form of a Fatras, a medieval French verse form defined particularly by its eleven-line strophe where the first and last lines become an introductory couplet.

'Fatras'
Variants on the original form.

'The Green Line'
The last six lines are reworked tweets from journalists reporting from the front line during the Gaza – Israel conflict, November 2012.

'A Vision of Sula Sgeir'
Sula Sgeir is an island in the North Atlantic. Since the sixteenth century, at least, men from the Ness district of the Isle of Lewis have sailed to Sula Sgeir annually in order to hunt guga (baby gannet) as a vital source of food. The tradition continues today. This poem is for Donald S. Murray.

'Seanair'
Seanair is Gaelic for 'grandfather'.

'Reflections'
"how beautifully sail the ships / we have missed" — derived from a line in a poem by Jules Laforgue: "How picturesque they are, the trains we've missed…" (*Derniers Vers,* poem ten).

Acknowledgements

Many of these poems, or versions of them, first appeared in
Poetry (Chicago), *Poetry Salzburg Review, Envoi, Gutter, Northwords
Now, Shearsman Magazine, The Ofi Press Magazine* (Mexico),
New Linear Perspectives, Ink Sweat & Tears, Shadowtrain and *From
Glasgow to Saturn*.

My grateful thanks to the Scottish Book Trust for their
continuing support through the New Writers Award scheme,
which made this collection possible. Special thanks to Jim
Murdoch, Elizabeth Horsley, Morgan Downie, and Holly
Hopkins at Eyewear Publishing, for their skilled and perceptive
comments on many of the poems in this collection. Most of
all thanks to my husband, Jamie McCready, without whose
unending love and support these poems would never have been
written.

EYEWEAR PUBLISHING